10/19
940.1 Git

# TOTALLY GROSS HISTORY™

# THE TOTALLY GROSS HISTORY OF
# MEDIEVAL EUROPE

**MARTY GITLIN**

rosen publishing's
rosen central®

Published in 2016 by The Rosen Publishing Group, Inc.
29 East 21st Street, New York, NY 10010

Copyright © 2016 by The Rosen Publishing Group, Inc.

First Edition

**Library of Congress Cataloging-in-Publication Data**

Gitlin, Marty.
The totally gross history of medieval Europe / Marty Gitlin. — 1st ed.
   pages cm — (Totally gross history)
Includes bibliographical references and index.
ISBN 978-1-4994-3766-9 (library bound) — ISBN 978-1-4994-3764-5 (pbk.) —
ISBN 978-1-4994-3765-2 (6-pack)
1. Middle Ages—Juvenile literature. 2. Europe—Social conditions—To 1492—Juvenile literature. 3. Europe—Social life and customs—Juvenile literature. 4. Hygiene—Juvenile literature. 5. Civilization, Medieval—Juvenile literature. I. Title.
D117.G58 2016
940.1—dc23

2015025265

*Manufactured in the United States of America*

# CONTENTS

# INTRODUCTION

It is true that many aspects of life in medieval Europe were gross and disgusting. People were dirty. Homes were filthy. Streets were filled with human and animal waste. Garbage floated on waterways. Rats and fleas brought disease. Medical science often did more harm than good. Food could be wretched.

But one must understand the times to appreciate the struggles of those who lived in them. No aspect of society was as advanced as it is today. History and the limits of knowledge explain much about medieval times.

One major problem was the world of medicine. Most people did not trust it to cure illness and disease—and for good reason. Those who practiced medicine (including barbers!) did not prove themselves able to make the people who came to them well.

Their methods were not based on sound principles gained through research. Too many loved ones died despite receiving treatment for anyone to believe in the medical profession. The beliefs of the medical profession were rooted in old Greek ideas that had never been proven by science. The result was that few were cured and many died.

But for millions in medieval Europe, even advancements in medicine would not have mattered. The Catholic Church was a dominant force. Many people believed that illness and disease were punishments from God that no medical treatment could cure.

A family in a typical one-room medieval cottage shared its home with livestock and boiled water in the middle of the room.

This belief was especially true when the Black Death killed an estimated one-third of the population of Europe in the 1300s. Folks tried to use black magic and superstition to keep death from their doorsteps. They simply did not understand why so many were dying in their homes and on the streets. Medical research had not caught up with reality.

That is because science and education, in general, were so far behind. The people of medieval Europe were mostly rural.

Cities were in decline by around 800. Most folks spent their entire lives tilling the soil. Their daily existence was consumed by simply feeding their families and avoiding the hardships of the times. Sickness and premature death were constant concerns. But society had not figured out how to prevent them.

Then there was war that brought more death. Horsemen called knights served their kings in battle. A series of conflicts, called the Crusades, between Christians of western Europe and Muslims, began in the late eleventh century and continued for about two hundred years. The Crusades resulted in many deaths and an even more disgusting Europe. Knights did not believe in cleanliness. That, too, contributed to the dirt and filth of the times.

City life emerged again around 1050. The poor sanitation in the cities and towns of medieval Europe resulted in filthy streets and waterways. It eventually led to the Black Death and millions of dead from Italy to Russia.

The plague left those still alive wondering if they, too, were soon to die. But it also helped advance medical science and sanitation. The success of those efforts helped Europe recover and become a healthier and cleaner place.

# CHAPTER ONE

# FILTHY FOLKS

Modern families enjoy having cats in their homes. They are fun to play with. They make nice pets. But folks in medieval Europe did not think of their cats as just furry friends. Their cats had an important purpose. They worked to catch the mice and rats that spread disease in the home.

Modern families look forward to a warm bath or shower after a hard day of work. But some peasants in the Middle Ages never took a bath, even if they spent all day toiling and sweating in the hot sun. They just grew dirtier and smellier.

People today take toilets for granted. But a thousand years ago, many dropped their

This oil painting shows an old woman emptying a chamber pot filled with human waste into the street below.

7

waste into chamber pots. Some people just emptied them out the window and into the street!

These are just a few disgusting examples of everyday life in medieval Europe. One must understand, though, why it was so hard to keep bodies and homes clean.

## BATHING AND HYGIENE

First of all, running water was rare. Only the wealthy and some people who lived in convents were lucky enough to have it. Everyone else had to fetch water from nearby wells or streams. One can only imagine how long it would take to collect enough water to fill up a bath.

Nobody had hot running water. Those who wanted to heat their water did so in a large kettle over the fire in their homes.

The effort of gathering water made bathing rare for peasants. It is believed it was only done outdoors in good weather. Jeffrey L. Singman, who wrote a book about daily life in medieval Europe, reported that the peasants in the French village of Montaillou were not known to have bathed at all!

When families did bathe, one member would follow another into the tub. The children would soak in the filth of those in the tub before them. The oldest member of the family would bathe first, and the youngest would bathe last. Hence the old expression "don't throw the baby out with the bath water."

Hand washing was easier and more frequent. Peasants washed their hands and faces in the morning and during other times of the day. It was important for them to wash their hands before meals because their food was handled with their fingers.

Only royalty and the fortunate few were lucky enough to have running water and proper cleansing stations in medieval Europe.

Bathhouses in larger cities gave folks a better chance to stay clean. In 1292, there were twenty-six bathhouses in France. The German town of Frankfurt-on-the-Main boasted at least fifteen bathhouses in 1387. Most people in that era, however, lived in villages and rural areas, and they rarely bathed.

Those circumstances meant dirty people wearing dirty clothes, even in medieval London. There were no paved roads in that British city. People walked on bare earth covered with human and animal waste. Food and dead animals also lay rotting on the ground for people to step on.

At the same time, many folks did not wash their outer clothes. They wore the same outfits day after day and merely shook or brushed them off. Underwear was rinsed more often and hung to dry over a pole.

Medieval women did take care to keep moths from their dresses. They aired their clothing outside on sunny and dry days. They learned not to store their dresses in a chest after airing on cloudy days. The cooler air would invite vermin.

Teeth cleaning was easier than bathing for most folks in medieval Europe. But bad breath was common because of the lack of toothpaste and mouthwash. Some effort was put into cleaning teeth. In the 1100s, people in Wales used green hazel twigs and wool cloths to do the job.

## EDICT FROM EDWARD

British king Edward III tried to help clean up London in 1362. He ordered that butchers be banned from killing animals, such as pigs, oxen, and bulls, within the city.

He explained, "The air of this city is very much corrupted and affected [from the] putrefied [animal blood] running down the streets and the bowels cast into the Thames [River] whence abominable and most filthy stinks proceed." The king added that "sickness and many other evils" had become a huge problem in London.

Butchers were supposed to take their animals out of town to slaughter them. Those caught slaughtering them in London were to be jailed for a year. But that did not stop some butchers from continuing to do what was illegal.

Dental hygiene was not considered important during that time. The result was that teeth often simply rotted out. The bad teeth were pulled without the use of a painkiller, which caused great agony. There were no false teeth or dentures during that period. Those who lost their teeth could not get them replaced.

## TOILETS AND WASTE MANAGEMENT

Toileting was even more difficult. Most people had no easy way to rid themselves of their waste. Individuals rich or fortunate enough to live in castles or convents used garderobes. Garderobes were rooms that featured a bench with a hole in it. Some garderobes had no screens or doors. People would relieve themselves into the hole and wipe with straw, moss, leaves, wool, or linen rags. The waste would then slide down a chute into a pit, moat, or cesspit. People known as gong farmers would clean the waste away. But before that could be done, the waste could create an enormous stench.

The situation of gong farmers was gross enough, but it was not as disgusting as the plight of medieval

During medieval times, human waste and other debris were cast into the hole of a castle's garderobe, seen here from the outside.

peasants. Their toilets were buckets in the corner of a room.

After they relieved themselves, they sometimes tossed the waste into a larger container behind their homes, the forest, or a nearby river. Yes, the same river from which they retrieved water for cooking and bathing! It is no wonder they feared that bathing could make them sick.

Some homes did have a privy—a small shed near the house. The chamber pots full of human waste were sometimes dumped into the privy, which was built over a cesspit. Folks not only dumped their pee and poop into the cesspit but also threw a variety of household garbage into it.

The cesspit was then often emptied into the fields to fertilize the crops! The result was a lack of raw vegetables in the home. They had to be cooked because human waste as fertilizer made them unhealthy to eat raw.

Even the healthiest diets would not have saved many from disease and death in medieval Europe. They often could not avoid the filth that made living in those times so disgusting.

# CHAPTER TWO

# BRAINS AND LUNGS, ANYONE?

I magine sitting down for a meal. You ask what you are having for dinner. The reply: sheep intestines, lungs, brains, boar guts, and stomachs. These main dishes are what rich people often ate in medieval Europe.

## THE MEDIEVAL MENU AND DINING HABITS

Only the wealthy were deemed fit to hunt such animals as rabbit and wild boar. None of the animal was wasted.

Pudding made from sheep innards, such as heart, liver, and lungs, is called haggis. An English cookbook in the Middle Ages featured a recipe for haggis, which remains popular in Scotland.

Although what wealthy people often ate was gross, they were urged to use per-

Haggis is a pudding made from sheep innards and usually boiled in the sheep's stomach. It was eaten by wealthy Scottish people during the Middle Ages.

13

table manners. One thirteenth-century verse urged diners to do the following before and during a meal:

- Let your fingers be clean and your fingernails well-groomed.
- Do not touch your ears or nose with your bare hands.
- Do not clean your teeth with a sharp iron while eating.
- Refrain from belching at the table.
- Know that it is forbidden to put your elbow on the table.
- Do not gnaw a bone with your teeth.

Not all foods eaten in medieval Europe were disgusting. Studies have shown that medieval diners were daring in their diets. They tried a wide variety of fowl and fish. Meals included starlings, vultures, swans, cranes, herons, peacocks, porpoises, seals, and whale. Among the popular vegetables were turnips, parsnips, carrots, peas, and fava beans.

The difference between noble and peasant fare in medieval Europe was huge. Nobles often made an event out of their meals. They even sometimes placed live birds in a pie. The birds would surprise guests by flying out of the pie when it was cut open. The famous poem titled "Sing a Song of Sixpence" had a reference to this form of entertainment. It included the line "four-and-twenty blackbirds baked in a pie."

Much of what was served by the nobility at dinner was displayed to impress guests. Bear paws, for instance, were considered an exotic delicacy.

Certain foods were eaten for particular reasons. A French cookbook claimed that hedgehog meat cured those who had problems urinating. Sea otter was considered seafood, so it could be eaten on Fridays by Catholics who were not allowed to eat meat.

Other foods, however, were simply gross. Some in the Middle Ages ate sheep genitals! One recipe called for the genitals to be cleaned, roasted, and spiced with cinnamon, ginger, and pepper.

Another disgusting dish was roast cat. Stray cats were considered pests in medieval cities. So they were sometimes captured and eaten.

One recipe called for the cat's head to be cut off and thrown away. Its claim was that "eating the brains will cause

## GETTING A LITTLE SPICY

Some foods were certainly gross in medieval Europe. But folks used plenty of spices to make sure they were not bland.

People could thank many of the kings, knights, and crusaders—including many women—for these spices. These individuals traveled 3,000 miles (4,828 kilometers) to Middle East trade centers to bring back unusual spices used in other cultures. They went to such countries as Egypt, Syria, and Iraq. Traders from those nations had brought spices in from such places as India and Persia. The spices were then carried across the Mediterranean Sea to Italian ports.

Among the spices introduced to folks in medieval Europe were black pepper, cinnamon, cloves, nutmeg, ginger, garlic, caraway seed, and mustard seed.

him who eats them to lose his senses and judgment." For some strange reason, the recipe also asked for the cat to be buried underground for twenty-four hours before cooking.

Among the most common foods eaten mostly by wealthy people was lamprey. The eel-like fish looked disgusting but had a meaty texture and was an easy fish to raise in medieval Europe. King Henry I of England was said to have died from eating too much lamprey in 1135.

The eel-like lamprey was a popular main dish among the royalty and nobility in medieval Europe.

The nobility served food to their guests in hollowed-out bread dishes called trenchers. The leftover bread was often stale and moldy. However, the hosts believed they were being generous when they gave away that disgusting bread to the peasants. After all, the peasants were often used to eating bad bread. It was common for grains to become moldy in the fields. That mold found its way into the flour and bread eaten daily by the peasants.

Eating at home could indeed be dangerous. City dwellers who could afford it sometimes visited cook shops, which provided safer foods. *The Canterbury Tales*, written by Geoffrey Chaucer around 1387 to 1400, includes a reference to a woman sent off to buy a goose and loaf of bread.

Despite such issues, few in medieval Europe went hungry. There were brief periods of famine for the poor. A temperature change in the 1200s known as the Little Ice Age was harsh for those who tilled the land and did not have enough money to buy

This fifteenth-century print shows a group of medieval peasants enjoying a meal outdoors, although the food apparently did not agree with one fellow.

food. But for the most part, everyone was well fed. Spices were not used to hide rotten food. They were used as they are today—to improve the taste.

## FRESH FRUITS AND VEGETABLES AND STORING FOOD

The folks in medieval Europe did not always have good instincts about food. For instance, the wealthy ate virtually no fresh fruit. Fruit packed with vitamins, such as apples, oranges, peaches, strawberries, cherries, and melons, were available. However, the nobility viewed uncooked fruit with suspicion.

Wealthy people left fruit for the peasants to eat. As a result, the nobles were without vitamin C and fiber in their diets, which led to such physical problems as rotting teeth, skin disease, scurvy, and rickets.

A lack of understanding caused problems for millions during that period. In most cases, they were simply not advanced enough. There were no refrigerators and freezers to store meat and vegetables. Meat could be preserved only outside in frozen temperatures.

An Italian visiting Russia in the 1400s marveled at the food market on the banks of a frozen river. He noted that entire skinned cows and pigs were preserved long enough to be sold three months after they had been killed. They were shown to potential buyers placed standing straight up as if they were alive! That sight would have been a strange one to a visitor. But the ability to preserve meat and vegetables in any way was a step forward in medieval Europe.

# CHAPTER THREE

# THE BARBER WAS A SURGEON

Picture yourself going into a barbershop. The barber sits you down in the chair. He places a sheet over you. He fetches scissors and asks you what you would like done.

You reply that you want your hair shorter all the way around. Then you tell him your tooth hurts and you want it pulled. Because you also felt some pain in your knee, you want him to extract some blood from it.

This situation might sound foolish to you today, but it was not to the folks in medieval Europe, where barbers were also surgeons. Their methods of curing people were based on ideas now considered ridiculous and even scary.

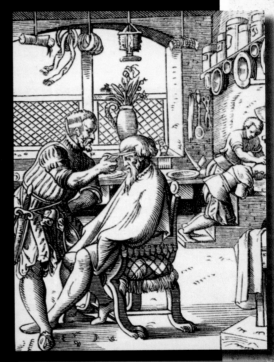

The medieval barber would not only cut hair, but he would also perform bloodlettings and other surgical practices, such as amputating limbs.

19

## THE BARBER IS A DOCTOR

Doctors were well respected in society. They learned their craft at a university. Their task was simply to diagnose a problem. Just as today, the job of providing medicine was left to a druggist. Quite unlike modern society, though, the surgeon was not required to attend college.

That circumstance did not matter to most people. They could not afford doctors anyway. So they visited local barbers, who did far more than trim hair. They performed surgery, often on men wounded in war. Many barbers had no formal training.

### THE BIRTH OF BARBER POLES

People in modern European society know when they have come across a barbershop. The shops have red-and-white poles in front of them. But many do not know that the tradition of displaying red-and-white poles started in medieval times.

Barbers from that era proudly displayed such poles in front of their shop to show that they performed bloodlettings. The red reflected the color of the blood. The white reflected the napkins used to clean up during bloodlettings.

American barber poles also have blue stripes in them. One theory is that blue was added to give the poles the same colors as the American flag.

## MEDICAL PRACTICES

Among barbers' most common chores was bloodletting. It was believed that ridding an ailing body part of blood would cure illness and disease.

This notion was born centuries earlier. A Greek named Galen believed that the body was comprised of four properties: choler, phlegm, melancholy, and blood. According to Greek medicine, illness was a result of imbalance in those properties. Cures could be achieved by fixing that imbalance, which was sometimes through bloodletting.

Medieval scholars wrote a great deal about ailments, symptoms, and cures centered on the belief in the four properties. The course of study to become a doctor in medieval times was long and demanding.

But in 1163, the church forbade monks and priests from practicing bloodletting. The job was left to those whom everyday people could afford and trust. That person was the barber, who performed a variety of functions from 1100 to 1500. He pulled teeth, performed surgery on minor wounds, and amputated limbs.

He would also place leeches on the body to extract blood. He would rub the skin with sugar water, milk, or blood. That addition would entice the leech to bite down and start sucking blood.

Leeches could be applied to the rear end to cure such diseases and illnesses as hepatitis, enteritis, and infections of women caused by childbirth. Leeches could be placed in the

A medieval person who was sick, such as this woman, often placed leeches on the body in failed attempts to cure whatever was ailing her or him.

nose to relieve nosebleeds. A barber might have even attached a string to a leech to lower it into the tonsils of a patient.

Wealthier folks in medieval Europe were not free from gross medical practices. Doctors in those times would give patients a series of tests. Among them was checking their pulse with a sand clock to measure time. Another test was checking urine by sniffing and even tasting it for sediment and sugar.

During the Middle Ages, a doctor who failed to examine urine could be exposed to public beatings. Patients often carried their urine to doctors in colorful flasks held in wicker baskets. They sometimes had their urine shipped to doctors so it could be examined.

Such primitive medical thinking made matters worse. People had plenty to worry about in regard to health. Poor diets, terrible sanitation, and rare bathing resulted in sickness and disease. So did an inability to protect oneself from the cold of the winter and heat of the summer.

## DISEASE, INJURY, AND SICKNESS

Dirt and filth resulted in vermin carrying disease or people contracting disease directly. The hard work of farmers and laborers caused widespread arthritis. Infrequent bathing meant skin disease and leprosy, which was common but not understood.

Personal injury was also a major problem. Every home featured an open fire, which often caused burns. The difficulty of labor for farmers in rural areas and workers in the city resulted in frequent injuries. War and violence meant death and destruction. Even sports, such as soccer, were played with brutality that sometimes killed participants.

Many did not live long enough to experience such medical problems. Childbirth was a time of danger for both mother and infant. According to Singman, a study of Italy in the 1400s revealed

14.4 deaths for every 1,000 births. Though that rate is still low, it is twice as high as in the poorest countries of the modern world.

Even those that made it past birth often did not survive childhood. Disease and primitive medical care resulted in many early deaths. During the 1200s, about one of six babies died in their first year, and just one in four made it to the age of five. About one-third of all people at that time never reached the age of twenty.

Knowledge of sickness and disease had not reached the point for people to understand it. Many Christians felt such physical problems were God's punishment for sin or the result of witchcraft. They might believe a sick person was possessed by demons.

They also did not see medicine as a way to cure anyone. Their feeling was that only prayer, help from saints, or atoning for sins could make a person well.

One might understand that thinking. The medical world had not proven itself capable of curing ill and diseased folks. It would take many years for people to be convinced that medical science was the answer.

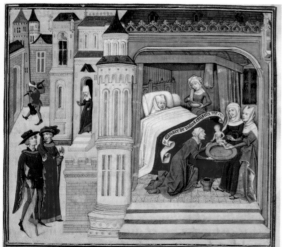

The birth of a baby in medieval Europe was fraught with danger, and instead of doctors, midwives delivered infants. Many times both the mother and the baby did not survive childbirth.

# CHAPTER FOUR

# SICKENING STREETS AND STREAMS

People in medieval Europe had to deal with their gross homes. They were too hot or too cold. They were filthy. Rats darted around their rooms.

But things got no better when they ventured out. The streets, lakes, and rivers were overflowing with human and animal waste. People tossed urine-filled containers out their windows. Garbage sat in the streets or floated in rivers. It was disgusting.

## URBAN CONDITIONS

Only about 10 percent of all Europeans during that time lived in cities, such as London, Paris, and Rome. The Middle Ages were a period of growth for such urban areas. However, the horrible conditions resulted in the death rate exceeding the birth rate.

The cities stunk. One Paris native left for a while and returned around 1200. He noticed the

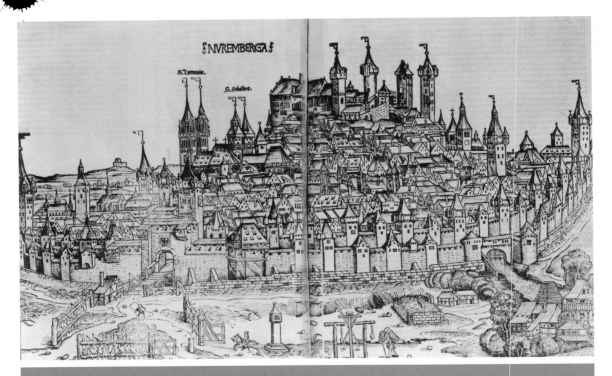

Among the many filthy cities of medieval Europe was Nuremberg, Germany, which is seen in this woodcut from the fifteenth century. The moat, which often became a sewer, and the drawbridge are depicted at the left.

stench when he came back. He wrote that one must leave Paris and return to understand how bad it smelled.

The homes of folks in medieval cities had cesspits and rubbish pits for human waste and garbage. The residents might dump them into the streets, into rivers, or into forests. Because drainage was so bad, the streets were subject to flooding. Rivers might overflow. The result was that the waste often poisoned the drinking water.

Not that the animals cared. They simply added to the filth. Horses, oxen, and donkeys were everywhere because they were

# JUST BEING POLITE

The idea of what was polite changed in medieval Europe. The filth and stench in the cities made men a bit more protective of women.

One such courtesy helped men protect women from getting hit with human and animal waste or garbage thrown out of upper-floor windows. Men escorting women positioned themselves closest to the street. That's where garbage would normally hit the ground.

A distinguished Dutch scholar named Erasmus also had ideas about politeness. He wrote that it is rude to greet someone who is urinating or pooping.

Soldiers also had their own ideas about right and wrong. The creed of many fighting men was that it was bad to clean themselves. They equated filthiness with manliness. That is one reason why streets and waterways became so dirty during that time.

needed for transportation. Pigs and dogs often strayed from homes and joined them. They would even enter other houses and attack infants!

In 1131, a French prince destined to be king was riding along in Paris when a pig startled his horse. The startled horse fell to the ground, landing on the prince and killing him.

Such animals were only part of the problem. Rats and mice were common sights in the streets. So were flies, fleas, and lice that carried disease—and eventually the plague in 1347 that killed millions.

Medieval London might have been worse than Paris because none of its streets were paved. The people in that British city

Folks could not get relief from dirt and filth by venturing out in the streets, which were stinky and disgusting. In this print, a woman can be seen throwing garbage from a window.

produced 50 tons (about 45 metric tons) of human and animal waste each day. Much of that wound up in the streets and waterways. People walked on dirt roads filled with such excrement, as well as rotting animals and food.

It was illegal to empty chamber pots filled with human pee and poop into the streets. But many individuals paid little attention to the law. They were not about to haul those containers outside the city, so they simply dumped them out their windows.

Author Terje Tvedt, who wrote a book about the history of British waterways, noted that some people did not bother urinating in a pot. Around midnight on one cold night in January 1325, a London resident named John Toly had to relieve himself. So he got out of bed and stood naked in an upper-story window. He leaned over to pee onto High Street and plunged to his death!

Sanitation elsewhere was a huge problem. Among the cities that struggled to keep clean was Florence, Italy. Early twentieth-century writer and historian Roberto Davidsohn considered the city to be beautiful. But his research found that it was disgusting during medieval times. He wrote that it was "foul, ill-kept and ill-smelling." He added that folks ignored laws intended to stop them from dumping waste into the streets.

## MUCKRAKERS AND FILTH CONTROL

City officials in London could certainly understand that problem. Workers there called muckrakers were hired to rake up the muck. Their job was to clean the streets, which had become so full of waste and garbage that people could no longer pass through. The work was incredibly revolting. But muckrakers were paid much better than the average working person.

A fast-moving cart holding dead bodies during the Black Death races through a smelly London street and scares pedestrians.

The Thames River was also filthy. But that was not the fault of the folks of London. The entire city had just twelve rubbish carts to place garbage. That was not nearly enough to hold all the trash people wanted to dump. So, much of it ended up in the river. Even the rubbish from the carts was often dropped into the Thames.

The people of medieval Europe were aware that terrible sanitation caused disease. Nevertheless, the resources in the cities were not enough to control the filth.

Even the air was sickening. Diseases were blamed on the foul odors and disgusting vapors rising up from the filth in the streets, as well as the decaying food and animals. In 1290, a religious order called the Carmelites complained that the stench of the nearby waterway had caused the death of its friars.

Many decrees issued by the city and the king in the 1200s and 1300s addressed the problem of disease. They called for measures to solve the pollution problem at its source. British king Edward III in 1355 ordered a study of the ditch surrounding a prison. The ditch was filled with human waste and garbage. The prisoners had contracted disease because of the infected air and incredible stench.

By that time, the diseases contracted by folks throughout medieval Europe had become an epidemic. What became known as the Black Plague had begun.

# CHAPTER FIVE

# THE BLACK PLAGUE

One might think there were enough fleas and rats and filth in medieval Europe to cause a plague by themselves. Yet research shows that the killer known as the Black Death began in China.

## RATS AND THE BUBONIC PLAGUE

Sometime around 1300, the climate became hotter and drier in central Asia. Millions of black rats scrambled to find food. They found food in the camps of nomadic herders who lived on the plains and began to spread disease. When those people moved through China with their grains and other food, they attracted infected rats and fleas. The disease finally reached the ports, where rats and fleas boarded ships.

By the early 1300s, China had become a world trade center. But it had also become a center for

Black Rat.

Hewitt

Length to the tail 7 Inch

The bubonic plague, also called the Black Death, killed about one-third of the European population and got its start from diseases spread by rats.

the bubonic plague. Rats there became infected by bacteria. Fleas fed off the rats and carried the disease to people.

Once individuals were affected, they experienced fever and a painful swelling of the lymph glands. The plague also caused red marks on the skin, called buboes, that turned black.

## THE PLAGUE ARRIVES IN EUROPE

The first Europeans to contract the disease were Italian sailors from merchant ships. They visited China in October 1347. By the time they arrived back in Sicily, many of them were already dying. Soon the plague had spread to the city and countryside.

The Italian sailors were driven out of town, but the damage was already done. Death was everywhere. Parents abandoned their dying children in fear of contracting the disease. Lawyers dreading death refused to visit sick people seeking to make out their wills. Monks and nuns who cared for the sick began dying as well. Bodies were left in empty homes with nobody around to bury them.

Most people in medieval Europe lived in small villages near grain fields. The tiny houses were made of sticks, mud, and straw roofs. Infected rats easily invaded them and built nests. In bigger cities, the rats feasted on waste and garbage in the streets.

Death came quickly. Some folks would get sick in the afternoon and die in the evening. By the following summer, the plague had spread all over Europe. First it hit Italy. Then Spain. Then France. Then England. Then Germany. Then Norway. Then Russia.

## THE EFFECTS OF THE BLACK DEATH

The disease had become known as the Black Death because of the black spots it produced on the skin. The medical world of the times was not advanced enough to find a cure.

The fleas that carried the disease struck every spring to kill new victims. Within five years, an estimated twenty-five million people were dead. That was one-third of the entire European population. Smaller outbreaks of the disease continued for centuries. The plague did not disappear until the 1600s.

In this fifteenth-century artwork, monks are shown caring for the sick, who have buboes on their bodies, during the bubonic plague. Treatment proved futile and often caused those close to the diseased to be infected, too.

Some villages and towns were hit harder than others. Nearly every person in the German city of Lübeck was struck down.

The effects of the disease on the victims were horrible. They would begin to vomit blood. They would often become frantic

# THE RHYME OF DEATH

It is uncertain when children first danced to the famous nursery rhyme "Ring Around the Rosy." But what is certain is that the words referred to either the Black Plague of the 1300s or 1600s in London.

The words tell a story of people dying in the streets: "Ring around the rosy...A pocketful of posies...Ashes, ashes...We all fall down."

"Rosy" is the color of the red rash in the shape of a ring on the skin, otherwise known as a bubo. The posies are the sweet-smelling flowers carried by medieval folks, who believed the foul smells in the city brought death. The words "ashes, ashes" refer to the dead bodies that had been burned. "We all fall down" simply referred to those who dropped dead in the streets.

from fever and fear. Boils developed and grew larger all over their bodies. The victims' coughs would spread the sickness to anyone unlucky enough to be nearby. The swelled lymph nodes eventually burst.

The sickness usually lasted about three days. By the fourth day, the victims were dead. By the time one wretched soul was gone, others with whom he or she came in contact were already dying.

The winter brought hope that the Black Death was over. The cold weather killed fleas and made rats inactive. They were no longer spreading the disease. Nonetheless, with the spring came new fleas, active rats, and death to millions.

LA STERILITE LA FAMINE ET LA PESTE SEMBLENT CONCOVRIR A L'ENTIERE DESTRVCTION DE PARIS

The dead and dying were everywhere in the streets of Paris during the Black Death period of the fourteenth century.

People in fear for their lives remained in their homes, but they, too, fell ill. Only the stench of their rotting bodies signaled their death to neighbors. Others dropped dead in the streets. The cities and villages were filled with corpses.

When the Black Death first struck, friends and families prepared coffins and funerals. Within weeks, the death count rose so fast that officials were forced to dig mass graves. However, there was not enough cemetery space to bury all the dead, so huge pits were dug and the bodies tossed in. The trenches were topped off by a layer of dirt, onto which more bodies were placed.

Even that was not enough. Pope Clement VI had the entire Rhone River blessed so corpses could be dumped into it.

Nobody could understand why it was happening. The plague had many peasants believing they were being punished by God. Some resorted to magic charms and spells. Others burned incense or other herbs. They believed that the incredible stench of the dead victims was causing more to die.

Church and public officials tried more logical measures to stem the tide. They attempted to prevent the sick from infecting others by walling off their homes. The areas of Europe where that was done did report a decrease in deaths. Pope Clement VI even sat between two large fires in his home. He understood that excess heat destroys bacteria.

## MEDICAL CURES

The professors of medicine at the University of Paris lost all sense of logic. They wrote a report on how the disease started. It claimed the disease began when the alignment of the planets soaked up vapors from the earth that were spread by wild winds. It stated that the foul air penetrated to the heart and corrupted the spirit.

European doctors suggested cures that were equally silly. They told folks to run away as the plague approached and avoid excess exercise and bathing. They urged people to burn incense and carry flowers. They advised smelling strong odors from latrines to overcome the plague vapors. They proposed wearing religious medals and holding papers with magic words on them such as "abracadabra."

It is no wonder that the Black Plague killed so many people. The medical world had not advanced far enough in medieval times to deal with it.

However, with setbacks come steps forward. Medicine in Europe later became more open to scientific observation and evidence. Hospitals provided treatment rather than a place to die. City officials became more aware of the importance of sanitation. Garbage began to be collected off the streets.

Medieval times were totally gross and disgusting. In spite of that, they helped people gain an understanding of how to live better.

# GLOSSARY

**amputate**  To remove a limb, such as an arm or leg.

**arthritis**  A constant and painful inflammation of a joint.

**bloodletting**  The practice of removing blood through a vein.

**convent**  A community of people devoted to a religious life.

**corpse**  A dead body.

**decree**  A new order or law.

**enteritis**  Inflammation of the intestines in the human body.

**epidemic**  A widespread disease affecting many people.

**excrement**  Waste matter from the body.

**famine**  A situation in which there is a shortage of food.

**genitals**  The sexual organs.

**hepatitis**  Inflammation of the liver, generally caused by a virus.

**leech**  A blood-sucking worm.

**leprosy**  A disease caused by bacteria affecting the skin and nervous system.

**noble**  A wealthy, high-ranking person.

**primitive**  An early stage of development.

**rickets**  A childhood disease marked by soft bones due to a lack of vitamin D.

**scurvy**  A deadly disease caused by lack of vitamin C.

**vermin**  Small rodents and insects that carry disease.

# FOR MORE INFORMATION

American Historical Society: Medieval Academy of America
17 Dunster Street, Suite 202
Cambridge, MA 02138
(202) 544-2422
Website: https://www.historians.org/about-aha-and-membership/affiliated-societies/medieval-academy-of-america
This educational museum promotes research in all aspects of the medieval world.

The Arizona Center for Medieval and Renaissance Studies
Arizona State University
P.O. Box 874402
Tempe, AZ 85287-4402
(480) 965-5900
Website: https://acmrs.org
The activities of this organization, which studies medieval culture, include summer studies in Europe for students and supporting research and lectures on the Middle Ages and Renaissance periods.

The British Museum
Great Russell Street
London WC1B 3DG
England
Website: http://www.britishmuseum.org/explore/cultures/europe/medieval_europe.aspx
The British Museum preserves and exhibits artifacts of distant British history, including medieval times.

Camlann Medieval Village
10320 Kelly Road NE
Carnation, WA 98014
(425) 788-8624
Website: http://www.camlann.org
This living history museum re-creates the common experiences
of living in a fourteenth-century rural village in Somerset,
England.

The Canadian Society of Medievalists
Department of English
Carleton University
1812 Dunton Tower
Ottawa, ON K1S 5B6
Canada
Website: http://www.canadianmedievalists.ca
This organization focuses on research into medieval studies
and brings together scholars and students who study the
medieval period.

The Medieval Institute
Western Michigan University
Kalamazoo, MI 49008-5432
(269) 387-8745
Website: http://wmich.edu/medieval
An organization established in 1962, this acclaimed institute
focuses on instruction and research into the Middle Ages and
provides students with programs about medieval culture.

Metropolitan Museum of Art (MMA)
1000 Fifth Avenue
New York, NY 10028
(212) 535-7710
Web site: https://www.metmuseum.org/toah/hi/te_index
    .asp?i=15
The MMA features medieval art and artifacts, an arms and
    armor division, and a collection of medieval musical instru-
    ments. The Cloisters museum and gardens is a branch of the
    museum that also exhibits medieval artifacts and is located in
    Fort Tryon Park in northern New York City.

The National Museum of the Middle Ages
6 Place Paul Painleve
Paris, France
Website: http://www.musee-moyenage.fr
The National Museum of the Middle Ages features artifacts and
    information on the history of medieval France.

## WEBSITES

Due to the changing nature of Internet links, Rosen Publishing
has developed an online list of websites related to the subject of
this book. This site is updated regularly. Please use this link to
access the list:

http://www.rosenlinks.com/TGH/Europe

# FOR FURTHER READING

Allen. Kathy. *The Horrible, Miserable Middle Ages*. Mankato, MN: Capstone Press, 2011.

Barber, Nicola. *Medieval Medicine*. Chicago, IL: Heinemann-Raintree, 2012.

Bredenson, Carmen. *Don't Let the Barber Pull Your Teeth: Could You Survive Medieval Medicine?* Berkeley Heights, NJ: Enslow Publishers, 2011.

Edgar, Frank. *Medieval Times: Grades 5–8*. Quincy, IL: Mark Twain Media, 2012.

Jeffrey, Gary, and Nick Spender. *Crusades*. St. Catherines, ON: Crabtree Publishing, 2014.

Langley, Andrew. *Medieval Life*. New York, NY: DK Publishing, 2011.

Lassieur, Allison. *The Middle Ages: An Interactive History Adventure*. Mankato, MN: Capstone Press, 2009.

Levy, Janey. *Plague: The Black Death (Doomed!)*. New York, NY: Gareth Stevens Publishing, 2015.

Levy, Janey. *20 Fun Facts About Women of the Middle Ages*. New York, NY: Gareth Stevens Publishing, 2015.

Macauley, David. *Castle*. Boston, MA: Houghton Mifflin Books for Young Readers, 2013.

MacDonald, Fiona. *You Wouldn't Want to Be a Medieval Knight*. London, England: Franklin Watts, 2013.

Mattern, Joanne. *Medieval Times: England in the Middle Ages*. Huntington Beach, CA: Primary Source Readers, 2012.

Miles, Liz. *Meet the Medievals*. New York, NY: Gareth Stevens Publishing, 2014.

Shapiro, Stephen, and Ross Kinnaird. *It's a Feudal, Feudal World: A Different Medieval History*. Toronto, ON: Annick Press, 2013.

# BIBLIOGRAPHY

Aden, Josh. "Gross Medieval Foods You'd Never Want to Eat." Allday.com. Retrieved June 17, 2015 (http://allday.com/post/356-gross-medieval-foods-youd-never-want-to-eat).

Berger, Darlene. "A Brief History of Medical Diagnosis and the Birth of the Clinical Laboratory." Retrieved June 16, 2015 (http://www.academia.dk/Blog/wp-content/uploads/KlinLab-Hist/LabHistory1.pdf).

Constitutional Rights Foundation. "The Black Death: A Catastrophe in Medieval Europe." Retrieved June 12, 2015 (http://www.crf-usa.org/bill-of-rights-in-action/bria-26-2-the-black-death-a-catastrophe-in-medieval-europe.html).

Gay, Lance. "Research Reveals Medieval Diet Was More than Meat and Gruel." *Pittsburgh Post-Gazette*, February 17, 2003. Retrieved June 17, 2015 (http://old.post-gazette.com/healthscience/20030217medieval0217p3.asp).

Gilbert, Rosalie. "Clothing Care: Traditional Remedies and Recipes for Care & Management of Clothing." Rosalie's Medieval Woman. Retrieved June 17, 2015 (http://rosaliegilbert.com/clothingcare.html).

History Undressed. "History of Hygiene: Bathing, Teeth Cleaning, Toileting & Deodorizing." July 14, 2008. Retrieved June 16, 2015 (http://www.historyundressed.com/2008/07/history-of-hygiene-bathing-teeth.html).

Kirkham, Kevin. "Transcript of Gross Medieval Food." Prezi.com. March 19, 2014. Retrieved June 15, 2015 (https://prezi.com/jd43kwxoe2mb/gross-medieval-food).

Lawrence, Leah. "Bloodletting: An Early Treatment Used by Barbers, Surgeons." HemOnc Today. February 10, 2008. Retrieved June 16, 2015 (http://www.healio.com/hematology-oncology/

news/print/hemonc-today/%7B630731c4-d1a3-4d77-94b9-8a2850da4f0e%7D/bloodletting-an-early-treatment-used-by-barbers-surgeons).

Medieval Life and Times. "Medieval Fruit." Retrieved June 15, 2015 (http://www.medieval-life-and-times.info/medieval-food/medieval-fruit.htm).

"Medieval London: 10 Disgusting Facts." *Telegraph*, April 5, 2011. Retrieved June 14, 2015 (http://www.telegraph.co.uk/culture/tvandradio/8421415/Medieval-London-10-disgusting-facts.html)

Meissner, Daniel J. "The Black Death: Horseman of the Apocalypse of the Fourteenth Century." Retrieved June 14, 2015 (http://academic.mu.edu/meissnerd/plague.htm).

Middleages.net. "The Black Death: Bubonic Plague." Retrieved June 14, 2015 (http://www.themiddleages.net/plague.html).

Newman, Paul B. *Daily Life in the Middle Ages.* Jefferson, NC: McFarland & Company, 2001.

Singman, Jeffrey L. *The Middle Ages: Everyday Life in Medieval Europe.* New York, NY: Sterling Publishing, 1999.

Thorndike, Lynn. "Sanitation, Baths and Street-cleaning in the Middle Ages and Renaissance." *Speculum*, Vol. 3. No. 2, 1928. Medieval Academy of America. Retrieved June 17, 2015 (http://www.jstor.org/stable/2848055?seq=1#page_scan_tab_contents).

Tvedt, Terje. *A History of Water Control and River Biographies.* London, England: I. B. Tauris & Co., 2006.

Velton, Hannah. *Beastly London: A History of Animals in the City.* London, England: Reaktion Books, 2013.

# INDEX

# ABOUT THE AUTHOR

Marty Gitlin is an award-winning writer and author based in Cleveland, Ohio. He has written dozens of educational books for elementary school and middle school students about history and social studies. He spent seventeen years in the newspaper field and won more than forty-five awards, including first place for general excellence from the Associated Press. Several of his published works have been about European history, including one in the medieval realm about the history of the Vikings.

# PHOTO CREDITS

Cover, p. 1 Peter Adams/Taxi/Getty Images; p. 5 Christian Jegou Publiphoto Diffusion/Science Source; p. 7 National Trust Photographic Library/Bridgeman Images; p. 9 © Chronicle/Alamy; p. 11 Photo © Lucinda Lambton/Bridgeman Images; p. 13 Norman Pogson/Shutterstock.com; p. 16 British Library, London, UK/ © British Library Board. All Rights Reserved/Bridgeman Images; p. 17 Hulton Archive/Getty Images; p. 19 Private Collection/Ken Welsh/Bridgeman Images; p. 22 Science Source; p. 24 DEA/G. Dagli Orti/De Agostini/Getty Images; p. 26 Fotosearch/Archive Photos/Getty Images; p. 28 Private Collection/ © Look and Learn/Bridgeman Images; p. 29 © Art Directors & TRIP/ Alamy; p. 32 Time Life Pictures/The LIFE Picture Collection/Getty Images; p. 34 De Agostini/A. Dagli Orti/Getty Images; p. 36 De Agostini Picture Library/Getty Images; cover and interior pages Lukiyanova Natalia/frenta/Shutterstock.com (splatters), idea for life/Shutterstock.com, Ensuper/Shutterstock.com, ilolab/Shutterstock.com, Sfio Cracho/ Shutterstock.com, Apostrophe/Shutterstock.com (textures and patterns)

Designer: Michael Moy; Senior Editor: Kathy Kuhtz Campbell; Photo Researcher: Carina Finn

## DATE DUE

PRINTED IN U.S.A.